Contemporary Issues
in the American Economy

THE JOSEPH I. LUBIN MEMORIAL LECTURES

NUMBER 6

Edited by
Daniel E. Diamond

Contemporary Issues in the American Economy

The Joseph I. Lubin Memorial Lectures, 1989–1991

The Joseph I. Lubin Memorial Lectures
Leonard N. Stern School of Business
New York University

NEW YORK UNIVERSITY PRESS
NEW YORK AND LONDON

HC
106.8
.C6654
1992

NEW YORK UNIVERSITY PRESS
New York and London

Copyright © 1992 by New York University
All rights reserved

Library of Congress Cataloging-in-Publication Data
Contemporary issues in the American economy : the Joseph I. Lubin
memorial lectures, 1989–1991 / edited by Daniel E. Diamond.
p.   cm.—(The Joseph I. Lubin memorial lectures : no. 6)
ISBN 0-8147-1843-4
1. United States—Economic conditions—1981–   I. Diamond, Daniel
E., 1929–   . II. Series.
HC106.8C6654   1992
330.973′092—dc20   91-45578
                                                                    CIP

New York University Press books are printed on acid-free paper,
and their binding materials are chosen for strength and durabitity.

Manufactured in the United States of America

c   10 9 8 7 6 5 4 3 2 1

CONTENTS

v

PREFACE

Daniel E. Diamond

Dean, The Undergraduate College
Leonard N. Stern School of Business
New York University

The Joseph I. Lubin Memorial Lectures were established and funded in perpetuity through the generosity of the late Joseph I. Lubin, a distinguished business, philanthropic, and civic leader. Mr. Lubin wished to provide a public forum for the discussion and practical application of economic and management principles and theories.

Mr. Lubin, a graduate of Pace College and New York University's School of Law, was a cofounder and senior partner of the nationally known accounting firm Eisner and Lubin. A CPA, he was a major contributor to the accounting profession serving as chairman of the New York State Board of Certified Public Accountant Examiners, vice president of the New York State Society of Certified Public Accountants, and a member of the Council of the American

Institute of Certified Public Accountants. He was also active in other business areas, including serving as chairman of the board of the United Cigar–Whelan Store Corporation, the Pepsi-Cola Company, and the Phoenix Securities Corporation. In addition to other real estate holdings, in the late 1950s he purchased the Astor Hotel on Times Square. As a grade school student, he had worked at the hotel as a page boy.

Mr. Lubin's humanism and beneficent impact on our society was evidenced by his many interests and generous contributions. In particular, institutions of higher learning benefited from Mr. Lubin's largess. At New York University, in addition to establishing the Lubin Memorial Lectures at the Leonard N. Stern School of Business, he, together with the estate of his partner, Joseph Eisner, financed the Eisner and Lubin Auditorium at the University's Loeb Student Center. He made a major contribution to Pace University, which named its School of Business and Administration in his honor. In addition, he made sizable donations to the Hebrew University of Jerusalem, Syracuse University, and Yeshiva University's Albert Einstein College of Medicine.

Joseph I. Lubin served as a trustee of New York University and Pace College, as well as being an overseer at the Albert Einstein College of Medicine. In recognition of his generous benefaction and involvement, Mr. Lubin received honorary doctorates from Yeshiva University, Syracuse University, Pace University, and New York Law School. Moreover, Mr. Lubin served as a director of the Henry Street Settlement; Children's Village in Dobbs Ferry, New York; the New Rochelle Hospital; and the Union of American Hebrew Congregations. For some fifteen years, he was national treasurer of the United Jewish Appeal and the Joint Distribution Committee.

This book contains the Lubin Memorial Lectures presented at New York University's Stern School of Business in 1989, 1990, and 1991. They were respectively the sixth, seventh, and eighth in the series. The previous lectures were:

1984   The World Banking System: Outlook in a Context of Crisis
Andrew F. Brimmer, President of Brimmer Company, Inc., and Chairman of the Monetary Policy Forum

1984   The Deficits: How Big? How Long? How Dangerous?
Daniel Bell, Henry Ford II Professor of Social Sciences, Harvard University

1985 The Dollar, Debt, and the Trade Deficit
Anthony M. Solomon, Former Undersecretary of the Treasury, Former President and Chief Executive Officer of the Federal Reserve Bank of New York

1987 The Strategic Defense Initiative: Its Effect on the Economy and Arms Control
David Z. Robinson, Executive Vice President and Treasurer, Carnegie Corporation of New York

1988 A Perspective on the Changing Business and Financial Environment
John J. Phelan, Jr., Chairman and Chief Executive Officer, New York Stock Exchange, Inc.

The Lubin Memorial Lectures are made possible by the Joseph I. Lubin Fund, and this book by his daughter, Barbara Goldsmith.

ACKNOWLEDGMENTS

Appreciation and thanks are due to Amy Jessica Frank for her invaluable role in organizing and putting together the material for this book. We also wish to thank the staff of New York University Press for their editorial and technical assistance.

THE MEDIA AND THE CEO

Steven T. Florio

President and Chief Executive Officer
The New Yorker *Magazine, Inc.*

Remarks by Steven T. Florio
on the occasion of the annual
Joseph I. Lubin Memorial Lecture
20 February 1991

Leonard N. Stern School of Business
New York University

I'd like to begin my discussion of the news media with an analogy from show business. After all, the line between the news media and show biz has become rather blurred these days. In the 1920s, a disaster struck the motion picture industry. It wasn't the great Depression—it was the introduction of sound. Overnight some reputations took a nosedive, while others skyrocketed. Some actors who had been big stars in silent films turned out to have squeaky voices or heavy accents. Relatively unknown actors from the New York stage—people like Jimmy Cagney and Barbara Stanwyck—were suddenly in great demand for the simple reason that they could speak well. A change in technology had brought about the end of an entire world. And those who could not adapt to this new world went the way of the dinosaur.

In the 1980s, technology caught up with many executives in the business world, including myself. We became the focus of unprecedented scrutiny from the news media, particularly from television. And some of us were as unprepared for this new world as the silent picture stars were for the talkies.

Today it is no longer enough to put positive numbers on the balance sheet, or to offer shareholders an excellent return on investment. It is not enough to increase dividends, or even to set new records for profits and sales. All these things are still important, of course—they remain the traditional measures of competence. Almost equally important as the fact of competence, however, is the perception of competence. And many top executives are devoting more and more of their time these days to controlling that perception. Even the top brass of the military, it seems, have been forced to master the subtleties of image and media relations, as the war in the Persian Gulf demonstrated so vividly.

Who, after all, is the ultimate chief executive officer but a military commander in the field? Today, a man like General Norman Schwarzkopf, who commanded the allied forces in the gulf, has to be both military commander and media spokesperson. Schwarzkopf had to fight two wars—one for Kuwait and one for the hearts and minds of the American public.

Television has had a tremendous impact on the kind of information military leaders present. We are no longer given a linear recitation of troop movements and body counts. Instead, during the war in the Persian gulf, we saw videogame-type footage of smart bombs hitting their targets, and the general served as our master of ceremonies.

To do this job, it was important that the general look like a general, and General Schwarzkopf filled the bill. In addition to being a fine military officer, he projected the qualities we have come to expect from watching the films of Dean Jagger, George C. Scott, and John Wayne. In other words, he had to be able to act the role he played in real life. Whether we like it or not, these are the requirements that television has ushered in. And chief executive officers—or generals—who cannot meet these new demands will go the way of the silent matinee idol with the squeaky voice.

I'd now like to share with you a few ideas about chief executives and the news media—but first, a disclaimer. These are not the views of a media "maven" or some other kind of expert. My knowledge of the media is not that of critics like Pauline Kael or academics like Ben Bagdikian. My experience has been much more visceral. I know about the media in much the same way that a deer knows something about hunters.

Everyone knows that a change has occurred in the way we receive information and perceive the news. Think about the names of newspapers—the *Times,* the *Herald,* and most significantly, the *Mirror.* All these titles convey the idea that newspapers simply report the news. They are names from the nineteenth century, which believed in objectivity.

But let's examine the age of television. Almost immediately we encounter *Person to Person,* with Edward R. Murrow. The news was happening right in our living rooms. The reporter wasn't merely a faceless witness. He was a wise and trusted friend who helped us get to the bottom of things—or so it seemed.

From the 1950s on, television grew ever more personal. By the 1970s we were watching a show called *60 Minutes.* Has ever a medium more arrogantly announced its dominance? What that title implies is: "No matter how much news there is, we're going to cut it to fit our format. We're going to package it." Can you imagine a magazine called "60 pages—and not one paragraph more!"?

By the 1980s, we got the first television presidency. The president was an actor, and the camera was no longer just a witness to the event, it was the reason for the event. The news was a series of photo opportunities. Ideas became sound bites.

At the same time, cable came into its own. This enormously increased the number of channels and thus the need for programming. Aspects of life that were once treated broadly suddenly became objects of intense scrutiny.

The print media also changed. Mass publications like *Life* and *Look* fell victim to the mass appeal of television. We entered the era of specialty publications, and the number of pages devoted to areas of special interest, like business, greatly increased. Take all these trends together and they begin to seem like cross hairs intersecting over the heart of the corporate chief executive.

To top things off, these trends reached their peak at a time when American business had entered one of its most exciting and dynamic periods since the 1920s. In the 1980s and 1990s, business was where the action was, and where there's action, the media are sure to follow. As a result, the faces of business executives started turning up in such unlikely places as the front cover of the *New York Times Magazine*. And on any day of the week you could find some hapless CEO being raked over the coals in a television interview. I'll tell you the truth—a lot of us just weren't ready.

The year was 1989. The Exxon *Valdez* ran aground in Alaska. It was the worst oil spill in history and the American people wanted to know why it had happened. Where was Exxon Chairman Lawrence Rawl? He was safe behind his desk in New York. "Do you have any plans to fly to Alaska, Mr. Rawl?" "No," Rawl said, "the people on the scene are quite capable of handling it."

You know something? Rawl was probably right, but television wanted an image. It wanted Rawl dressed in a parka and mukluks like Sergeant Preston of the Mounties. It wanted a tough, but caring commander directing operations in Prince William Sound. Instead America saw a guy in a thousand-dollar suit passing the buck in New York and, in the very next shot, oil-spattered birds croaking on the beaches.

This is called "crisis management," and entire books and business school courses are devoted to its mysteries. A disaster has overtaken the company and the CEO must deal not only with the emergency itself, but with how the media are reporting the company's response to the emergency.

Let's look at somebody who did it well. Remember when strychnine started turning up in bottles of Tylenol? Johnson and Johnson Chairman James Burke was not too busy to take responsibility. He appeared on mass audience shows like *Donahue* and *60 Minutes*. And his message was simple: We are going to recall all thirty-one million bottles of the product. Was this strictly necessary to ensure public safety? Perhaps not. But from a public relations point of view it was vital. The recall sent the message loud and clear: ''Our company puts people above profits.''

Johnson and Johnson spent millions on the recall, but it got millions of dollars of goodwill in return. Exxon spent $1 billion on the cleanup, but its image has yet to recover from the impression of callousness created by inept management of the media.

My intention is not to criticize Rawl or Exxon, but to emphasize that the talents necessary for becoming a successful chief executive do not necessarily translate into an ability to handle the media. Some CEOs are like silent movie stars confronting the talkies. They've gotten to the top by means of exceptional abilities. They are good persuaders and leaders. They think, ''By God, I fought my way through the corporate jungle. I'm tough enough to handle a journalist.'' But they're wrong.

Let's take a look at what CEOs are up against when they deal with the press. I'd like to share a quote with you: ''A journalist is a kind of confidence man, preying on people's vanity, ignorance, or loneliness, gaining their trust and betraying them without remorse.''

Who does that sound like? Richard Nixon? Dan Quayle? Actually, it was Janet Malcolm, one of the finest journalists in America today, and those words appeared in the pages of *The New Yorker*. (Needless to say, it got her into a lot of trouble with other journalists.)

Ms. Malcolm was stating the negative side of the case. Let me, a nonjournalist, state the positive side. The men and women of the press are aggressive, intelligent, and highly trained. By the time a journalist gets to interview a CEO, he has put in many years at his profession. And he has achieved his position by making mincemeat out of the unprepared. The journalist comes to a story with an agenda.

If you are naive, you think that agenda is to learn the truth. If you are paranoid, you think it's to destroy your career. Neither of these scenarios is true.

A journalist wants to get a good story—it is as simple, and as complicated, as that. What makes a good story? Conflict, action, high drama, new information. That is what sells magazines and keeps jaded viewers from switching the channel.

A journalist wants to tell his story, not yours. You can forget about price-earnings multiples and organizational restructuring. That stuff goes on page six of the business section, if it gets in at all. The public wants *Dynasty* and *Dallas,* not Dun and Bradstreet, and it is the journalist's job to give this high drama to the public. That is why the media love to report corporate takeovers. They contain that all-important element of conflict. They can be portrayed as giant wrestling matches, with Kohlberg Kravis and RJR–Nabisco slugging it out instead of Killer Kowalski and Hulk Hogan.

Journalists also love corporate scandals. You will not see a headline in the *New York Post* trumpeting the fact that a major soft drink company has just announced a 50 percent increase in its dividend. But let someone find a dead mouse in a can of soda, sue for a million dollars, and win, and that makes the front page and the eleven o'clock news.

Which brings me to a central point—when a corporation makes the front page, it is rarely because of anything good. If a journalist approaches you rather than your media affairs people, it is because the issue is critical, and you had better be ready to deal with it.

If all this makes the press sound formidable, it should. The press is formidable and that is why, in the 1980s, chief executives with survival instincts began investing in media training for themselves and their staffs. The past decade witnessed explosive growth in the size and power of media consultants. (This was most visible in the political arena. Sometimes the 1988 election seemed to be nothing more than a battle between the Bush and Dukakis media teams.) Throughout the decade, firms like Burson-Marsteller and Reese Communications greatly expanded their media training services for people in the corporate world. It was simply a matter of supply rising to meet demand.

What do you learn in media training? Of course you learn the basics of handling yourself on TV. You spend hours in front of the camera while an expert corrects the way you sit, the way you talk, and your smallest gestures. Then you have the excruciating experience of watching a replay of the tape, and suddenly you have a whole new respect for Ed McMahon.

On a substantive level, you learn to simplify your responses. This stripping down of content contains some elements that are beneficial and others that are deeply disturbing. On the one hand, it is an excellent intellectual exercise to try to explain your position in the simplest possible terms. It helps you clarify your thinking. On the other hand, the inherent complexities of life tend to become blurred. Complicated issues are reduced to black and white or good guys versus bad. Of course, television and the media in general thrive on such oversimplification.

If coming up with a coherent position is beyond your intellectual capacity, the media consultants will supply you with one. They will poll public sentiment and hold focus seminars. They will tell you exactly what you should be saying to get the greatest approval of the greatest number. This is how idiotic campaign themes like ''no new taxes'' are born. It is also how disgusting campaign tactics like ''Willie Horton'' are unleashed.

Once you have boiled your position down to basic themes and message points, you are supposed to repeat them, and repeat them, and repeat them. You must avoid the temptation to elaborate. Television is no place to engage in Socratic dialogue. In many cases, your responses will be cut down to a single, seven-second sound bite. If you make the same point every time, you can be sure that your message will go out to the viewers. If you get bogged down in complications, the message will be blurred.

One of the most valuable things you learn in media training is how to say what you want to say rather than what the reporter wants to make you say. You learn how to respond to journalists and their techniques—for example, the "machine gun." This technique is a favorite of Dan Rather. The reporter asks you a question. Before you have a chance to respond, he follows it up with another question, and then a third. By the time he has gotten to the fourth question, you're tied up in knots.

Then there is the "I'm your friend" technique used so effectively by Barbara Walters. Here the reporter pretends you are two friends having a confidential chat and tries to lull you into forgetting that your answer is going out to a hundred million people.

Another gambit is what I call the "Perry Mason ploy." Raymond Burr used to confront the murderer on the witness stand by asking leading questions like, "Isn't it true you hated your wife for years? Isn't it true that when she turned her back you picked up the poker? And isn't it true you hit her again and again until she fell?" The murderer, of course, breaks down and says, "Yes, yes, I did it." If that murderer had had media training he might have said, "Wait a minute, Perry. You're not asking questions there. You're making statements. And those statements aren't true at all."

These techniques are only a few of the weapons that every trained reporter has in his or her arsenal. They seem transparent when discussed out of context. But in the midst of an interview they can be devastating, and you had better know how to counterattack.

When Dan Rather starts the machine gun, you have to know enough to say, "Hold it, Dan. You've asked five questions there and I'd like a chance to answer them all." When Barbara Walters says, "Just between you and me . . . ," you have to know enough to smile like the good friend she's making you out to be and then go back to your message, not hers.

Of course there is a heavy price to be paid for all

this competence in dealing with the media. One begins to see that glibness, rather than true thoughtfulness, is the key to successful image control. And one becomes aware that the media are to a large extent responsible for the cheapening of public debate in our society. This is not because news people are irresponsible or unskilled. On the contrary, they have never been more conscientious and highly trained. But technology itself has changed the nature of the national dialogue, just the way sound changed the movies. Things go faster, attention spans are shorter, and true thought requires time.

All of this poses a problem for a businessman who runs *The New Yorker*—a magazine that is one of the nation's leading cultural and literary institutions. When I came to *The New Yorker* in 1985, the magazine faced two distinct, and in some ways contradictory, problems with its image. On the one hand, some self-appointed experts were saying that *The New Yorker* had been an admirable magazine in its day, but that it had become irrelevant to today's generation. They pointed out that the magazine was losing ad pages, especially among advertisers who wanted to reach young urban professionals. On the other hand, some people warned that the management team I represented was going to wipe out everything that made *The New Yorker* unique and wonderful, that we were going to change it into another version of *Vanity Fair* or *GQ*. It was a classic case of ''damned if you do and damned if you don't.'' If we made no changes, we would be accused of being dinosaurs. If we made changes, we would destroy a great literary institution.

In actual fact, we made minimal changes on the editorial side, where we felt the magazine was strong, but we made massive changes in the magazine's antiquated business operation. The result, we felt, was a magazine that continued to maintain the highest editorial standards while offering advertisers an opportunity to reach some of the most sought-after consumers in America. Our problem then became how to communicate that message in ways that were not only effective, but also true and honest in the best tradition of *The New Yorker*.

Here are a few of the message points that we came up with:

The New Yorker is the best written, best edited, and best read magazine in America.

This was a basic point that we kept coming back to again and again. It reflected what we believe to be the simple truth.

The New Yorker is the magazine for the 1990s.

We pointed out that the current generation of readers was perhaps the best-educated group of people the world had ever seen and that *The New Yorker* beautifully satisfied their need for a magazine with serious editorial content.

The New Yorker is the blond cheerleader, who is also the class valedictorian.

This last is simply a one-liner I tossed out in an interview with Randall Rothenberg of the *Times,* but it made an extremely important point—that *The New Yorker* has tremendous popular appeal while at the same time being intellectually serious. In our case, the two are not mutually exclusive, they are mutually reinforcing.

At the same time, we took the unusual step, for *The New Yorker,* of putting ads on television. And for a while I became something of a fixture on cable business shows, making these points and facing down the challenges of reporters.

In 1989, the tide turned rather dramatically. In November of that year the Sunday *Times* business section asked a number of so-called experts "How do you fix *The New Yorker?*'' One suggested we should ''get glitzier,'' another said we needed to change our image, and a third pointed out that we were too staid to compete for advertisers. In fact, *The New Yorker* was doing better than ever, but let's face it—the image of this stately dowager mauled by the cruel modern world made a great, if not strictly accurate, story.

Less than a month—literally less than thirty days —later, the *Times* picked up on the fact that *The New Yorker* had posted a 5.4 percent gain in ad pages for the year, the largest gain in a decade, during a time when most other magazines were losing ad pages. *''New Yorker* staid no more,'' the headline trumpeted. Suddenly our image changed from old maid to old champ come back for another victory.

What's more, we were winning National Magazine Awards again. We won awards for excellence in fiction and reporting two years in a row. In the magazine business, that's like winning two Oscars two years back-to-back. The people who had been noisily predicting that we would compromise on quality suddenly got very quiet. In 1990—the worst year in thirty for the magazine industry—*The New Yorker* continued its success by gaining even more ad pages, increasing circulation, and winning two more National Magazine Awards.

Now, was this a triumph of image control? Did we convince the public that black was white and up was down, simply because we had refined our message points?

No. What happened was that the facts confirmed what we had been saying in the media. And I think that raises an important point: Yes, image is important. Yes, you have to learn to handle the media and control your company's image. You can no longer succeed without doing that. But business success is still the key. You still have to deliver, and you have to deliver a quality product. Image may be king, but truth is his throne. Pull the throne out from under the king—and he's just another man standing there.

Which brings me back to my analogy of the movies. The men and women of the silent screen may not have had beautiful voices, but they could act. They had real talent. When sound turned the film world upside down, the actors who made the most of the situation were not just pretty faces with good voices, they were wonderful actors too. The requirements for success had not simply changed, they had been upped.

In a similar way, the new dominance of image in

our public life should cause us to demand more from our leaders, not less. The bar has to be raised. As always, we need people who are competent in their jobs, but we need even more. We need people who can communicate. Image has not replaced competence, it has become an inseparable part of the definition of competence.

Ironically, the notion that image has replaced substance comes from the media itself. Journalists love to run thoughtful, disapproving pieces about the advent of the sound-bite and the photo-opportunity. Why? Because it makes a good story! But that does not make it the truth. Successful image control is not a substitute for talent and hard work. It is actually a new demand for excellence brought about by technology here at the end of this epic motion picture we call the twentieth century.

And if our society is to grow and prosper in the sequel our children will call the twenty-first century, we must develop people who can deliver both substance and image. People who realize that the two are not separate and distinct, but one and inseparable, constituting a quality which for want of a better word, I will call genius. Genius means different things in different ages, but in all ages it takes a touch of genius to see us through.

DEFICITS, DEBT, INTEREST, AND THE ENTITLEMENT EXPLOSION

John J. Creedon

Chairman of the Executive Committee of the Board of Directors
Metropolitan Life Insurance Company

*Essay by John J. Creedon
on the occasion of the annual
Joseph I. Lubin Memorial Lecture
21 February 1990*

*Leonard N. Stern School of Business
New York University*

CONTENTS

CHARTS
(Sources in parentheses)

5. National Debt (Office of Management and Budget)

6. Net International Investment Position—United States (U.S. Department of Commerce)

7. Interest on National Debt (Office of Management and Budget)

8. Composition of Federal Expenditures (Office of Management and Budget and U.S. Treasury)

9. Interest and Other Federal Expenditures (Office of Management and Budget)

10. Means-tested v. Non–means-tested Entitlement Spending (U.S. Treasury)

11. OASDI Benefit Payments, 1960–1989 (Social Security Administration)

12. Life Expectancy at Age 65 (Social Security Administration)

13. Social Security Contributions vs. Benefits *(Transactions of the Society of Actuaries)*

14. Social Security Programs as a Percentage of Taxable Payroll (Social Security Administration)

15. OASDI Trust Fund—Alternative II-b Projections (Social Security Administration)

16. Medicare Expenditures (Social Security Administration)

17. U.S. Health Care Expenditures, Selected Calendar Years 1969–1989 (Health Care Financing Administration and U.S. Department of Commerce)

18. Total Health Care Expenditures as a Percentage of GNP, 1987 *(Health Affairs)*

19. Medicare Contributions vs. Benefits (Metropolitan Life estimate)

20. Civil Service and Military Retirement Systems Expenditures (Department of Defense–Office of the Actuary and U.S. Office of Personnel Management)

21. Net National Savings Rate as a Percentage of GNP (Organization for Economic Cooperation and Development and U.S. Department of Commerce)

22. Poverty Status in the U.S. (U.S. Department of Commerce, Bureau of the Census)

23. Composition of Federal Expenditures, 1969–2029 (Office of Management and Budget and Metropolitan Life extrapolation)

TABLES
(Sources in parentheses)

1. Entitlement Program Expenditures, 1989 (Congressional Budget Office)

INTRODUCTION

I would like to thank Dean Diamond and the staff at the Stern School of Business for inviting me to give the 1990 Lubin Lecture.* It is a privilege and a pleasure to speak before such a distinguished audience. The invitation held special significance for me because I spent several years attending similar lectures while I was a student at NYU, in both the business and law schools.

*Note: Subsequent to the presentation of this lecture, the 1990 Social Security and Medicare Trustees Reports were published. The new data did not materially change any of the conclusions or recommendations expressed at the 1990 Lubin Lecture.

The subject of this lecture is the relationship between our federal government's budget deficits and the so-called federal entitlement programs—and a number of related matters. For anyone who is unfamiliar with the word "entitlements," the term refers to benefits the federal government pays to individuals through programs for the poor, such as Medicaid and Food Stamps, as well as other programs not designed for the poor, such as Social Security, Medicare, the Civil Service and Military Retirement systems, and a number of other programs.

To set the stage, I will briefly discuss a number of charts about budget deficits and then get into the subject of entitlements in a little more depth.

Federal Budget Deficits

Chart 1 shows our federal government's budget deficits since 1955.[1] With the exception of small surpluses in four years, there have been deficits in each of the last thirty-five years ranging from about $3 billion in 1955 to $221 billion in 1986 and they have grown particularly large in the last decade.

As we shall discuss in greater detail later and as shown in chart 2, especially since 1987, federal

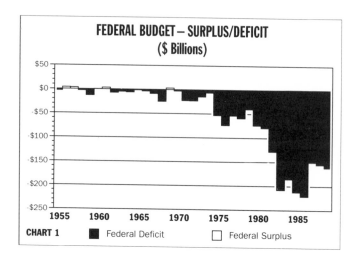

FEDERAL BUDGET – SURPLUS/DEFICIT
($ Billions)

CHART 1　　■ Federal Deficit　　□ Federal Surplus

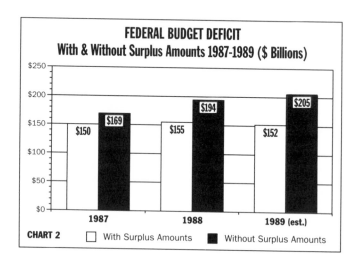

FEDERAL BUDGET DEFICIT
With & Without Surplus Amounts 1987-1989 ($ Billions)

CHART 2　　□ With Surplus Amounts　　■ Without Surplus Amounts

operating deficits have in fact been significantly larger than those shown in chart 1.[2] The reason is that the deficits reported by the government have been reduced by Social Security and some other so-called surplus funds, which are not surplus funds at all but are generally "reserves" needed for future obligations under various entitlement programs. For example, if you look at the 1989 deficit figure un-reduced by the surplus amounts, you will note that the government ran a deficit of over $200 billion in 1989—not the $152 billion you read about in the newspapers.

Chart 3 shows even more disturbing deficit pro-

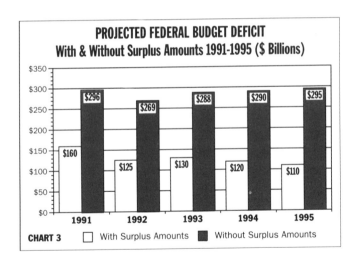

jections going out to 1995. Remember that the deficits are reduced primarily by Social Security surplus amounts, but there are also some other so-called surplus funds which, for example, in 1991 have been estimated as being $21 billion for Medicare, $20 billion for federal civil employee retirement plans, and $13 billion for military retirement plans.[3] As you can see, these numbers push the 1991 operating deficit up to almost $300 billion. And the savings and loan bailout will make the deficit worse.

Expenses, Not Tax Reductions, Are the Problem

Now, many people think that the reason for our federal budget deficit is that the income tax rate reductions in the Reagan years slowed the growth of federal revenues dramatically. Chart 4, I believe, disproves that view. From 1979 to 1989, the cumulative percentage increase in expenditures outpaced that of receipts (127 percent and 114 percent, respectively), and both increases were far in excess of the 68 percent increase in the Consumer Price Index (CPI), a measure of cumulative inflation.[4]

In dollar terms, federal receipts increased by $528 billion, from $463 billion in 1979 to $991 billion in

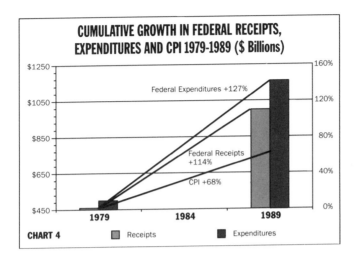

CUMULATIVE GROWTH IN FEDERAL RECEIPTS, EXPENDITURES AND CPI 1979-1989 ($ Billions)

Federal Expenditures +127%

Federal Receipts +114%

CPI +68%

CHART 4 — Receipts — Expenditures

1989. The problem is that federal expenditures increased by an even larger $640 billion, from $503 billion to over $1.1 trillion. Our major problem during the 1980s was that government expenditures continued to grow more rapidly than government revenues. This is the trend that must be reversed.

The National Debt

The aggregate amount of federal budget deficits from 1955 to 1989 (net of interest on the debt and unreduced by the ''surpluses'') totaled almost $2 trillion.[5] And, of course, to ''pay for'' the deficits the government must borrow money and pay interest on the debt, which brings us to chart 5 showing the federal government's outstanding debt over the last thirty-five years.[6] In 1955, the national debt was about $275 billion.[7] It now exceeds the astronomical sum of $3 trillion, more than a tenfold increase since 1955 and almost twelve thousand dollars for every man, woman, and child in our country.

In addition to their domestic consequences, another way to evaluate the significance of our budget deficits is to look at our net investment position,

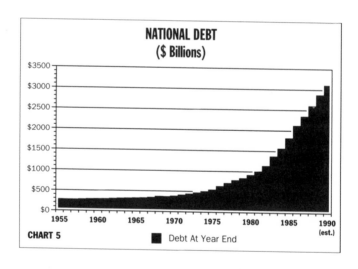

CHART 5

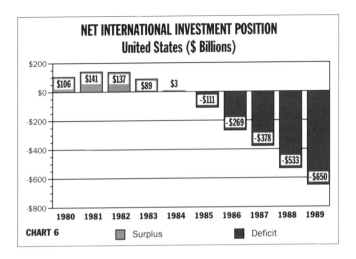

NET INTERNATIONAL INVESTMENT POSITION
United States ($ Billions)

CHART 6 — Surplus — Deficit

which is a relative measure of American investment abroad and foreign investment in America. As chart 6 shows, our country moved from being the largest creditor nation in the world at the beginning of the 1980s to being the largest debtor nation by the end of the decade.[8]

Interest on the National Debt

The interest paid on the national debt, as shown in chart 7, has quite naturally grown with the debt itself, from $5 billion in 1955 to $169 billion in

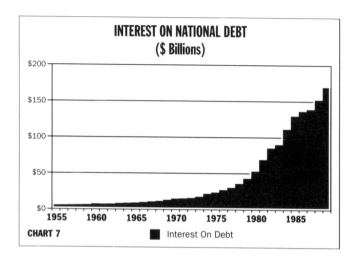

INTEREST ON NATIONAL DEBT
($ Billions)

CHART 7 — Interest On Debt

1989.[9] Interest on the national debt alone is now larger than all federal expenditures in 1967. If there is an encouraging side to this picture, it is that as a percentage of GNP, the federal budget deficit— even omitting annual Social Security and similar "reserves"—has gone down from a high of 6.3 percent of GNP in 1983 to about 3 percent in 1989. But I am not encouraged!

Budget Deficits: A Serious Problem

I believe continuing federal budget deficits, together with the growing national debt and the interest obligations that the deficits generate, are our country's most serious economic problem. If we are to remain a leading world economic force, the government must stop spending more than our income—and to me that means reducing the budget deficit to zero and building budget surpluses so as to reduce the national debt.

A most disconcerting aspect of the recent large budget deficits is that they have been occurring during times of relative peace and prosperity when we should be able to control our expenditures. One other significant comment about controlling expenses is that usually we are not talking about reducing expenses in the aggregate but rather reducing the rate of growth in expenses.

How to Distribute the Economic Pie

This brings us to what I regard as the primary question we should be asking ourselves today, which is: as a matter of social policy, how would we as a country like to see the federal economic pie distributed both now and, to the extent we can influence it, in the future?

GOVERNMENT EXPENDITURES

Some Trends

So now let's look at how the federal government has been spending our money. Chart 8 compares federal expenditures in 1969 with those in 1989.[10] It breaks expenditures down into four major categories: defense, entitlements, interest, and all other.

Obviously, during this twenty-year period, there were substantial increases in the dollar amounts of all four categories. But what is interesting is the changes in the percentages of total federal expenditures for each of the categories. As chart 8 shows, in 1969 defense expenditures amounted to $83 billion or 45 percent of all federal expenses. By 1989, defense expenditures had increased to $304 billion, but had been reduced to 27 percent of all federal expenditures.

In contrast, entitlement expenditures amounted to $59 billion or 32 percent of total federal expenditures in 1969. By 1989, however, entitlements totaled $536 billion or 47 percent of all expenditures. Thus, in that twenty-year period the relative percentages of defense and entitlements of all federal expenditures were reversed. Now this "reversal"

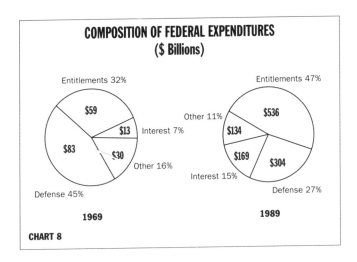

CHART 8

has positive aspects. It's better to spend on butter than on guns. But we must understand that entitlements have become the "big ticket" item among all federal expenditures.

Similarly, interest payments increased from about $13 billion or 7 percent of the total in 1969 to $169 billion or 15 percent of the total in 1989. Again, in contrast, all other federal expenditures such as spending for education, roads, bridges, law enforcement, drug control, the environment, and research increased from $30 billion to $134 billion, but decreased from 16 percent to 11 percent of all federal expenditures. In fact, as chart 9 shows,

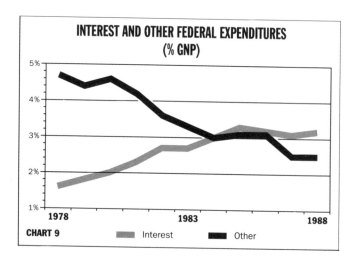

INTEREST AND OTHER FEDERAL EXPENDITURES (% GNP)

CHART 9 — Interest — Other

starting in 1984, our country began to spend more on interest payments than it spends on research, infrastructure, education, and all other programs included in the "other" category I just mentioned.[11]

You might ask why chart 8 begins with the year 1969 rather than some later point in time. The main reason is that twenty years gives a relatively long perspective. It is true, however, that the percentage spent on each category may vary significantly depending on the year with which you choose to begin. For example, if we looked only at the Reagan years, entitlements as a percentage remained about the same (47 percent), defense increased from about 23 percent to 27 percent, interest on the debt increased from 9 percent to 15 percent, and the "all other" category decreased from 21 percent to 11 percent.

Again, the fundamental question we need to ask ourselves is whether this is the way we want the federal government to spend our money.

Entitlements

I mentioned earlier that entitlements break down into two major categories: those that are means-tested (essentially for the poor) and those that are

---

ENTITLEMENT PROGRAM EXPENDITURES, 1989 ($ Billions)

MEANS-TESTED		NON-MEANS-TESTED	
■ Medicaid	$34	■ Social Security	
■ Food Stamps	13	- OASDI	$231
■ Supplemental Security		- Medicare	97
Income	12	■ Civil Service Retirement	
■ Aid to Families with		System	38
Dependent Children	11	■ Military Retirement System	20
■ Child Nutrition	3	■ Unemployment	
■ Guaranteed Student Loans	3	Compensation	15
■ Other	8	■ Farm Price Supports	13
		■ Other	36
Total Means-Tested	**$86**	**Total Non-Means-Tested**	**$450**

TABLE 1   Note: Totals may not equal the sums of the rounded components.

non–means-tested (mostly for the elderly in our society—regardless of their financial need). Table 1 shows most of the major entitlement programs and the amounts spent for each in 1989.[12]

As chart 10 shows, in 1989, entitlement spending for the poor amounted to $86 billion or about 16 percent of entitlement spending, while non-means-tested programs (not for the poor) amounted to $450 billion or 84 percent of such spending.[13] While programs for the poor can undoubtedly be improved, they are a relatively small part of federal expenditures and do benefit the needy in our society, so I'd like to concentrate primarily on non–

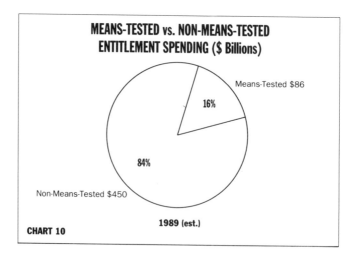

MEANS-TESTED vs. NON-MEANS-TESTED ENTITLEMENT SPENDING ($ Billions)

Means-Tested $86

16%

84%

Non-Means-Tested $450

1989 (est.)

CHART 10

means-tested programs—specifically Social Security, Medicare, and the Civil Service and Military Retirement systems—although some of my comments also apply to other entitlement programs.

Social Security [14]

The largest entitlement program is Social Security. It started in 1937 on a "pay as you go basis." A payroll tax of 2 percent (1 percent each for employers and employees) on a maximum of $3,000 of wages was more than enough to cover the benefits paid to retirees and survivors of covered workers. Since 1937, the combined employee/employer payroll tax rate has increased from 2 percent on a maximum of $3,000 of wages to 15.3 percent on $51,300. Since 1966, a designated part of the payroll tax has been used to finance Medicare as well as the basic Social Security program.

Chart 11 shows the benefits paid over the years for Social Security. [15] In 1960, Social Security benefits amounted to $11 billion. In 1989, the program provided $227 billion to about thirty-nine million beneficiaries and constituted 42 percent of total entitlement spending.

Let's look at some of the reasons for this phe-

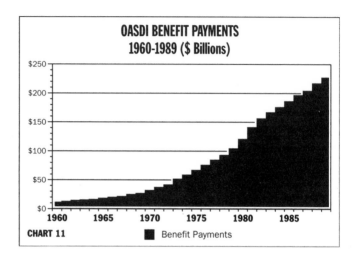

OASDI BENEFIT PAYMENTS
1960-1989 ($ Billions)

CHART 11 ■ Benefit Payments

nomenal growth. First, people are living longer, which is certainly good. Chart 12 shows that life expectancy at age sixty-five is now 16.9 years compared with 12.7 years in 1940, an improvement of 4.2 years or 33 percent.[16] This means that benefit payments are paid to more retirees and for a longer period of time.

Second, the Social Security program has been liberalized over the years so as to provide more generous payments to beneficiaries (which is also good up to a point, and which, of course, has required higher payroll taxes). Third, and highly important, since 1975 Social Security has provided for

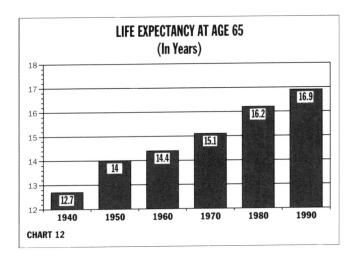

LIFE EXPECTANCY AT AGE 65
(In Years)

CHART 12

automatic cost-of-living adjustments (COLAs), which have added greatly to Social Security costs and are largely uncontrollable. In retrospect, this change may not have been so good—or, rather, it may not have been affordable. In the 1980s such COLA payments alone exceeded $300 billion.[17]

A few more observations about Social Security are worth noting. One point relates to the amounts received by Social Security beneficiaries. As chart 13 shows, current recipients (including wealthy people) receive about three to five times more in benefits than they contributed, plus interest.[18] Another observation: In 1955, there were 8.4 workers

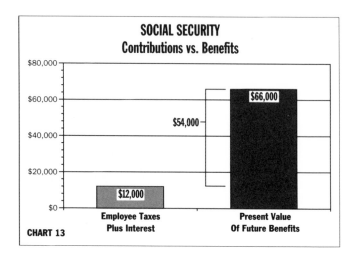

SOCIAL SECURITY
Contributions vs. Benefits

CHART 13

for every person receiving Social Security benefits.[19] Today there are only 3.3 and by 2030, the number is expected to go down to 2 to 1.[20] Thus, fewer workers are being taxed more to provide higher benefits for a growing number of retirees.

In fact, as chart 14 shows, the trustees of the Social Security system, who make optimistic, pessimistic, and medium forecasts, project that under the pessimistic scenario the combined employer/employee tax rate might have to be almost 50 percent to cover Social Security and Medicare by 2050.[21] Presumably, some Congressional action will be taken

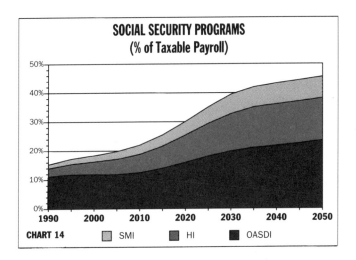

SOCIAL SECURITY PROGRAMS
(% of Taxable Payroll)

CHART 14   SMI   HI   OASDI

to avert this possibility, but chart 14 does show a worrisome trend line.

Social Security Reserves

A few words now and more later about the so-called Social Security surplus funds. In 1983, because annual Social Security payments to beneficiaries were expected to soon exceed payroll tax revenues, Congress increased payroll taxes with the result that "reserves" would build up to meet future benefit payments. These reserves represented a shift to a partial funding concept. Payroll taxes now being collected each year (as well as amounts to be collected for some years in the future) are in excess of the benefit payments being made. These excess payments are supposed to be put in a trust fund for future beneficiaries to be used when the time comes that benefit payments exceed payroll tax revenues. As you probably know, these "excess payments" received tremendous attention in the Congress during early 1990.

Inadequate Funding

As chart 15 shows, even with the 1983 changes, and assuming the trust funds are available for future beneficiaries, the trust funds are projected to peak at about $12 trillion (including interest) in the year 2031, and then decrease until they become completely exhausted in 2046.[22] In other words, it's going to take about forty-five years for the funds to reach a peak, but only fifteen years for them to become exhausted. Thus, Social Security is not being overfunded in an actuarial sense. In fact, if we valued the unfunded liability of the Social Security program for current workers only—as the private sector must do for private sector plans—the actuar-

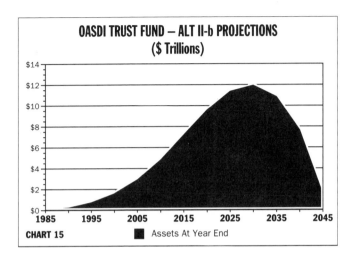

OASDI TRUST FUND – ALT II-b PROJECTIONS
($ Trillions)

CHART 15 — Assets At Year End

ial deficiency for Social Security is currently estimated to exceed $6 trillion.[23]

Reserves Are IOUs

A few other comments are relevant about the Social Security excess payments. They are not being directly deposited in a "trust fund" as that phrase is commonly understood. Rather, they are invested in special interest-bearing, nonmarketable securities of the federal government. Thus, trust fund assets might more accurately be viewed as governmental IOUs —that is, more government debt. The important

55

point is that the bulk of these funds is not being placed in productivity-enhancing investments, but is being used to fund current government operations.

Now let's go ahead to the year 2031. After that year, Social Security will be running large annual deficits, but the trust funds will have—at least in theory—a large balance. But this balance will not be available in cash. Rather, the fund will have IOUs which, hopefully, it will be able to cash in with the government.

But when the fund goes to cash in its IOUs, where will the $12 trillion come from? The government will have to decrease spending in other areas, cut back on Social Security benefits, raise taxes, or borrow more money.

Are Reserves Beneficial?

Whether the annual ''excess'' Social Security payments will have served a constructive purpose between now and 2031 will depend on how the trust funds are used. As time goes by, the total economic pie available to both active and retired workers must be proportionately larger if our standard of living is to be maintained or improved. For that to happen, the ''excess'' payments or trust funds must be ''invested'' so as to improve our productivity and help the economy grow. Otherwise, the net effect will simply be more inflation from far too much money chasing too few goods.

It is of interest to note that some other countries do use Social Security-type reserves to finance such projects as schools, hospitals, housing, and business.[24]

On- or Off-budget

One of the issues frequently raised in the current debate is whether the so-called Social Security and similar surpluses should be on-budget or off-budget. Currently, Social Security amounts are excluded from the budget totals except for the purpose of calculating Gramm–Rudman–Hollings deficit reduction targets. Remember that the deficit figure appears much smaller if the surplus amounts are included in the calculation.

Many people argue that the surplus amounts should be left off-budget for purposes of calculating the deficit because the amounts not only mask operating deficits, but also produce a false sense of security and reduce the impetus for deficit reduction in other areas of government. On the other hand, proponents of the ''on-budget'' argument say that if the surplus amounts are taken off-budget, it will be easier for proponents of Social Security expansion to demand even larger benefits—after all, if surpluses are off-budget, there would be the appearance of larger surplus amounts to spend.

I believe that, at the very least, the American people should know the truth about the surplus funds— that is, surpluses, as most people commonly use that term, do not exist and our federal operating deficit picture is much worse than some politicians would have us believe. And people are more likely to understand the exact situation if the ''excess'' funds are not used to make the deficits appear smaller.

Medicare

Let's turn now briefly to Medicare, which is the fastest growing entitlement program. Chart 16 shows the trend of Medicare benefit expenditures.[25] In 1989, Medicare provided $101 billion to about thirty-two million people and represented 18 percent of all entitlement spending.

The Medicare program consists of two parts. The Hospital Insurance program, often referred to as HI

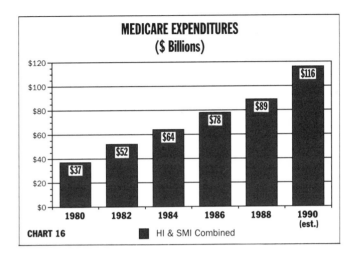

MEDICARE EXPENDITURES
($ Billions)

CHART 16   ■ HI & SMI Combined

or Part A, covers inpatient hospital and certain home health services. As I mentioned earlier, it is financed by a dedicated part of the payroll tax which now stands at 1.45 percent.[26] The Supplementary Medical Insurance program, usually called SMI or Part B, covers physician and outpatient services. It is financed from general tax revenues and insurance premiums paid by the beneficiaries.

Currently, some ''excess funds'' or reserves are being generated by the payroll tax for the Hospital Insurance part of Medicare. However, the projected financial situation is much worse than for the Social Security program. Under the ''moderate'' assumptions scenario, HI Medicare payments are expected to exceed the dedicated payroll tax revenues by 1995 and all reserve funds are expected to be depleted by 2005.[27] So some action on Medicare is necessary quite soon.

Of course, Medicare is part of the larger picture involving health care costs, which, as chart 17 shows, have skyrocketed in the past two decades, from $66 billion in 1969 to an estimated $599 billion in 1989.[28] Increased health costs are due to a variety of factors including improved technology, huge medical malpractice awards, drugs and other medical develop-

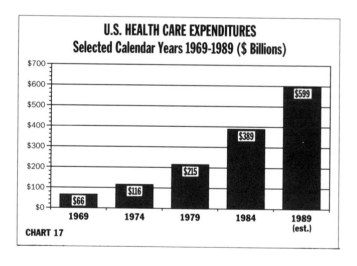

U.S. HEALTH CARE EXPENDITURES
Selected Calendar Years 1969-1989 ($ Billions)

CHART 17

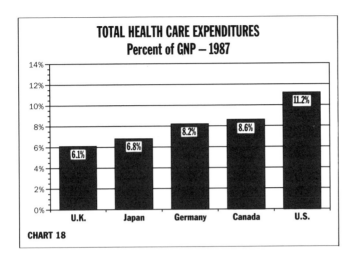

ments, longer life expectancies, and higher standards of living.

Chart 18 shows that the United States spends a larger share of its Gross National Product (GNP) on health care than any other industrialized nation.[29] It has been suggested that these comparisons may not fully be apples to apples since it is not clear that other countries include the same categories of expenditures in their totals as we include in ours.[30] However, in any event, only six countries in the world have a total GNP larger than what we spend for health care alone each year![31] With Medicare,

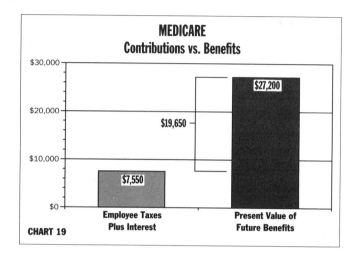

CHART 19

too, it is important to note that current beneficiaries receive much more from Medicare than they contribute—as shown by chart 19.[32]

Civil Service and Military Retirement Systems

The Civil Service and Military Retirement systems are the next largest non–means-tested programs. These programs provide retirement benefits to federally employed civilian personnel and members of the U.S. Armed Forces, respectively.

As chart 20 shows, as in the case of Social Security and Medicare, costs under these two programs

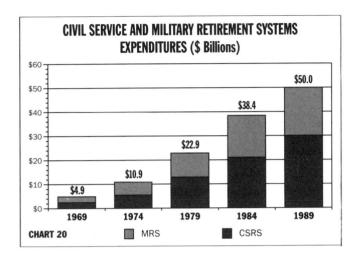

CIVIL SERVICE AND MILITARY RETIREMENT SYSTEMS EXPENDITURES ($ Billions)

CHART 20   MRS   CSRS

have been rising sharply.[33] In 1989, expenditures for the two programs combined totaled $50 billion, an increase of 920 percent over the $4.9 billion spent in 1969.[34] Last year, these programs constituted over 9 percent of entitlement spending.[35]

In part, these retirement program costs have been escalating because the systems have traditionally provided generous cost-of-living adjustments (COLAs). Aside from the costs, this practice can produce unfair results. For example, an active Civil Service employee working in a job filled by a retiree years ago could be making less money than the retiree receives in retirement benefits. This unfair-

63

ness results because the retiree receives payments adjusted annually by the CPI, while the active employee typically receives less than this amount in annual pay increases.

Moreover, the Civil Service Retirement System provides pension benefits which are more generous than many private sector plans. The cost of such benefits is estimated to be around 25 percent of payroll—substantially greater than is typical for the private sector.

Increasing costs under the Military Retirement System are partially attributable to the low average age of retirement for military personnel. Since the median age of retirement for career servicemen is about forty-three, retirement benefits are received for a long period of time.[36] Also, most military pensioners are eligible for Social Security and have second careers. This situation leads to the so-called triple dip—military pension, Social Security, and private pension payments.

DIFFICULT QUESTIONS

Some Economic Principles

Unfortunately (or perhaps fortunately), I am not an economist; some of my observations, therefore, may not withstand rigorous economic analysis, but I would nevertheless like to advance a few propositions.

• It is the total volume of goods and services produced by our country that is the basis for our standard of living.

• As part of an increasingly global economy our goods and services are in competition with those produced by other countries both as to quality and cost.

• Our ability to compete as a nation will depend, in part, on our investment in plants, equipment, and other facilities that improve our productivity.

• To the extent we can produce and invest in buildings, infrastructure, and other products that last into the future, we will be adding to the future economic pie for our children and grandchildren.

• Our cost competitiveness also depends, in part, on the nature, variety, and amount of the various elements contributing to our costs (including the cost of entitlements) compared with those of other countries.

• Savings are also an important part of the equation because they are the source of investment in productivity enhancements. And as chart 21 shows, the rate of saving has been much lower in the United States than in the United Kingdom, France, Can-

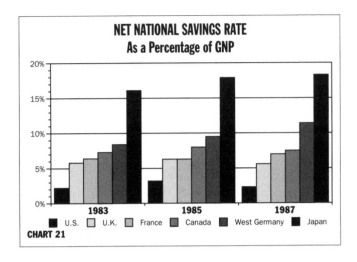

NET NATIONAL SAVINGS RATE
As a Percentage of GNP

■ U.S.   □ U.K.   ▨ France   ▨ Canada   ▨ West Germany   ■ Japan

CHART 21

ada, West Germany, and Japan.[37] We averaged a 2.9 percent rate of saving during most of the 1980s, while the other countries averaged 9.4 percent. Fortunately, the U.S. savings rate has been improving recently.

The Economic Pie Revisited

So where does all this leave us? Are the trend lines in the charts we have seen thus far satisfactory? Are we distributing federal government expenditures in a way that we think reflects good social policy? Are we content to pay an increasing percentage of our tax money for interest payments and a decreasing percentage for clean air, clean water, crime control, drug control, medical research, roads, bridges, and education? I believe the answer has to be a resounding no.

Will there be a large peace dividend as a result of easing international tensions? How large will it be? Should it be used in whole or in part to reduce the federal budget deficit? Or should it be used to finance entitlements at their present rate of growth or for some other government programs?

Should the Social Security payroll tax be reduced as Senator Moynihan has proposed so as to reduce the "excess funds" being generated as reserves for future liabilities? How about other similar reserves?

Another aspect of the question of how the federal economic pie is being divided concerns the extent to which our current entitlement spending policy protects all members of our society. Some suggest that one of the main problems with the nation's current policy is that it does not adequately protect the young.[38] They argue that massive amounts are given to elderly individuals through programs such as Social Security and Medicare without due regard to the financial needs of those individuals, while the needs of young families and children are often ig-

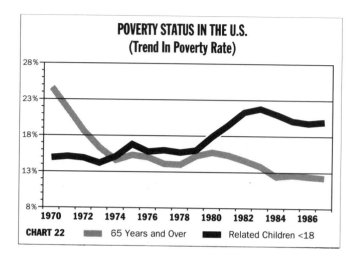

POVERTY STATUS IN THE U.S.
(Trend In Poverty Rate)

CHART 22   65 Years and Over   Related Children <18

nored. Chart 22 tends to support that position and shows that the number of elderly living in poverty has been decreasing, while the number of children living in poverty has been increasing.[39]

Another vivid example concerns health insurance. Medicare provides health benefit coverage to virtually all Americans over age sixty-five regardless of financial need. Yet, we are reported to have over thirty million people under age sixty-five without coverage and a good portion of them are children.

Use Peace Dividend to Reduce Deficits and Debt

I started out saying that I believe our federal budget deficits, our national debt, and our annual federal interest payments are our most serious economic problems and that we need to address them if our country is to remain strong. So any peace dividend, in my judgment, should be used in whole or significant part to help balance the budget and reduce the national debt.

Continue to Build Social Security Reserves

The Social Security "excess funds" pose a more complicated issue. In the final analysis, and as mentioned earlier, somehow they should be used to improve future productivity in our country—to improve our economic growth—and to provide a higher standard of living for future generations. They are now not being so used. Rather, they are being "loaned" to the federal government in return for IOUs. In theory, perhaps the result of these loans is that the government borrows less from other sources than it otherwise would have borrowed publicly, and an equivalent amount is invested by the private sector in productivity improvement. In fact, the trust fund moneys are probably encouraging less Congressional fiscal discipline, and the funds are being used to finance government programs that would not otherwise be undertaken. Senator Moynihan's proposal to reduce payroll taxes and reduce or eliminate the Social Security "surplus" may, in part, be motivated by this perceived need for more discipline.

While some arguments can be made for reducing the payroll tax, the review undertaken earlier of Social Security and Medicare leads me to a different conclusion. Both programs are growing at a rate that could result in their consuming a larger and larger part of the economic pie. Chart 23 shows what would happen if spending trends over the past twenty years continue into the future.[40]

Unless the trend line is permanently changed downward, extrapolated entitlements could grow to be an even "bigger ticket" item—they could comprise 69 percent of federal expenditures. In 2029 the country could be spending the remaining 31 percent of its budget on interest—whereas defense and all other items could extrapolate to a net zero.

To produce these figures, I just extended the trend

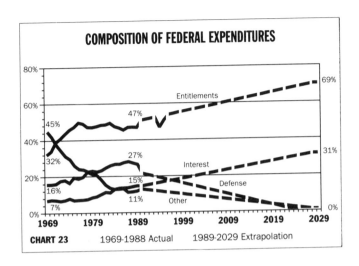

COMPOSITION OF FEDERAL EXPENDITURES

CHART 23   1969-1988 Actual   1989-2029 Extrapolation

lines out forty years. Certainly, government actions could be taken to alter the projected spending patterns. Nonetheless, the projections are dramatic and troubling, and demonstrate the need for strong action. In this situation, reducing the payroll tax simply does not make sense. Rather, the temporary Social Security excess funds must be channeled so as to improve national productivity.

One congressman has proposed that part of Social Security be privatized so that Social Security reserves would be invested directly in the private sector. As mentioned earlier, some countries do invest retirement reserves to enhance productivity.

President Bush has proposed that Social Security reserves be used solely to reduce the national debt, thus releasing equivalent funds for investment in the private sector. There are undoubtedly other creative possibilities, but cutting payroll taxes and thereby increasing budget deficits already out of control would not seem to be the judicious course.

CONTAINING ENTITLEMENT PROGRAM COSTS

One of the serious problems in controlling entitlement programs is that most of them are not part of the Congressional budget appropriation process. The programs have been established by laws and the level of payments (including, as mentioned earlier, cost-of-living increases under some programs) is uncontrollable in the budget process. Changes in the laws are necessary—changes that the Congress is too often reluctant to make.

What steps then might be taken to help contain the cost of Social Security, Medicare, and the Civil Service and Military Retirement systems?

Social Security

Tax Benefits More Broadly

One suggestion is to tax Social Security benefits once a retired employee receives benefits in excess of the employee's contributions into the system. Private pension plans are taxed that way. Such a tax would produce about $99.5 billion over the next five years and these funds could be used to reduce the budget deficit.[41] A portion of Social Security benefits is already so taxed; up to 50 percent of benefits are included in the taxable adjusted gross income for persons whose incomes exceed specified threshold levels ($25,000 individual; $32,000 married joint filer). So, we need only broaden the principle—leaving some exception for the poor.

Reduce COLAs

Another suggestion would be to reduce COLAs to something less than the full increase in the CPI—such as the CPI increase minus 1 percent or 2 percent. Few, if any, private pensions provide for full CPI adjustments. Such a change would have a dramatic effect on costs over time. Limiting COLAs to the CPI increase minus 2 percent for five years for Social Security and the Railroad Retirement program, for example, could result in savings of $73.4 billion.[42] In fact, a change in the CPI adjustment could result in Social Security being actuarially funded indefinitely into the future. Another alternative would be to skip or freeze the level of Social Security COLA payments for one or more years or to adjust the COLA every other year.

Increase Eligibility Age

Another possibility would be to increase the age of eligibility for Social Security payments. Under present law, the eligibility age for Social Security is scheduled to rise to sixty-seven for those attaining that age in 2027. Perhaps it should be increased even more to age seventy over the next twenty-five or thirty years. Improved mortality and the declining ratio of active workers to retirees suggest the desirability of such a change.

Some Means Tests

Other possible cost reductions might involve amending the system so that some ''means testing'' is used. Our wealthiest countrymen should be willing to accept some such change.

It is recognized that some of the suggested changes in Social Security would increase the so-called surplus funds that will be needed for future payments and would not immediately reduce budget deficits. Taxing more of the benefits received would, however, help to reduce budget deficits, and the other changes would help bring entitlement costs under control, which is necessary long range since Social Security is not actuarially funded.

Medicare

Change Eligibility—Means Tests

Here, too, the eligibility age should probably be changed so as to delay entry into the Medicare system. And perhaps there should be some "means testing" here as well.

Allocate Larger Percentage of Payroll Tax

Another suggestion would be to increase that portion of the payroll tax allocated to Medicare. If some of the changes suggested for Social Security were made, a portion of the payroll tax allocated to Social Security could be reallocated to Medicare—which is urgently needed.

More Cost Sharing

Other possibilities include: an increase in the premiums paid by Medicare beneficiaries, an increase in deductibles, and increased copayments or other ways of greater cost sharing by the beneficiaries and especially by those who can afford it. For example, the Congressional Budget Office recently projected that if the SMI premium, which is soon expected to cover somewhat less than 25 percent of the cost of benefits, was set to cover 25 percent of all benefits for 1991 and after, there could be savings of $13.2 billion over a five-year period. And if the premium was gradually increased to cover 30 percent of benefits by 1995, there could be an additional savings of $22.5 billion over the same period.[43] When Medicare was first enacted, the beneficiaries were expected to pay 50 percent of the benefit costs, but that has gradually been eroded.

Premium for Hospital Insurance

The government could also introduce a premium for Medicare Hospital Insurance benefits. Charging a premium of $10 per month, for example, could generate $3.9 billion in additional revenues each year.

The Civil Service and Military Retirement Plans

Reduce COLAs

Although legislation has been passed which provides for indexation to less than the full increase in the CPI in some of these retirement plans, the COLA change applies only to newer employees so that the savings effect is postponed far into the future. Applying the CPI less 1 percent or 2 percent to current retirees or postponing or freezing COLAs for a time might also be considered.

Realign Civil Service Plan with Private Sector Plans

Another suggestion would be to make benefits provided under the Civil Service program more comparable to those provided by the private sector—perhaps benefit costs could be limited to a fixed percentage of payroll costs.

Encourage Individual Saving

Subject to other action being taken to balance the federal budget, it would be desirable, long range, to encourage Americans to save more for their own retirement income and for their own retirement medical care so as to relieve pressure for constant expansion of Social Security, Medicare, and the Civil Service and Military Retirement systems. Better IRAs and a new IRA for medical care could be used for this purpose—again, however, only if the budget can be balanced.

TAX INCREASES HAVE NOT WORKED BEFORE—OTHER NEEDS

Many people argue that the only way to balance the budget is to increase taxes—and that may well be. If the past is any guide, however, when taxes are increased, the federal government immediately finds ways to spend the new tax money. Taxes were

increased many times over the past thirty-five years
—both because of changes in the tax laws and
because of growth in our economy—and yet during
that thirty-five-year period, there were only four
years with small budget surpluses. The record simply does not suggest that tax increases will be the
answer. Unless such increases are strictly restricted
to deficit reduction, they will simply be used to
initiate new government programs or expand existing ones.

And, of course, there are numerous ''needs'' in
our society still to be met. But unless we have a
period of relative ''belt tightening'' followed by
budget surpluses and reduced debt and interest payments, our long-range ability to grow the economy
to help meet those needs may very well be in jeop-
ardy.

POLITICAL WILL

Fortunately, it looks like defense spending can be
significantly reduced, at least in the near term—
although one sees widely different estimates as to
what reductions will take place. That reduction could
help balance the budget. But more will be neces-

sary. And the task seems impossible without greater restraint on the growth and expansion of Social Security, Medicare, the Civil Service and Military Retirement systems, and other entitlement programs that are not means-tested.

The major question then is whether we as a people and our legislative and executive representatives have the collective will to make the entitlement and other changes necessary to eliminate our budget deficits, reduce the national debt and interest payments, improve our savings and investments for the future, and leave an even stronger country to our children and grandchildren. The Congressional and executive record in recent years creates serious doubts as to whether our political process will allow appropriate action to be taken in the absence of a crisis. The recent experience with catastrophic medical insurance for the elderly illustrates the point. After passing a self-funding catastrophic care law, Congress quickly rescinded the law under pressure from the elderly.

Perhaps an economic crisis will arise and cause us to muster the political will for strong action. But an economic crisis may only deepen budget deficits and worsen the situation. In the absence of crisis, continuing deficits and larger and larger debt and interest, coupled with low rates of saving, might well slowly sap our economic strength and signal our decline as the leading economy in the world.

It is recognized, of course, that budget deficits, debt, and interest cannot be eliminated overnight without possibly adverse consequences on the economy and the country. We have been, after all, enjoying relatively good times while accumulating all this debt and interest. And, of course, I do not have to run for elective office, which adds another perspective. But we simply cannot as a country live beyond our means indefinitely; sooner or later our successors will pay for our profligacy. While there is undoubtedly a fine line to be drawn in taking actions to reduce budget deficits, it is submitted here that despite the deficit reduction as a percentage of GNP mentioned earlier, we are not making sufficient progress either in the entitlement area or generally, and the budget deficit picture is much worse than it appears.

SUMMARY AND CONCLUSION

In summary, the following major points have been made in this paper:

• Federal budget deficits not reduced by Social Security and other reserve-type funds are too high and, barring remedial action, are likely to persist at significantly above the $200 billion mark annually. And, of course, the savings and loan bailout will make the deficit much worse.

• The national debt now exceeds $3 trillion, and if the deficit reduction talks fail to make substantial progress, it could easily top $4.5 trillion by the end of the decade. In ten short years, we have moved from being the largest creditor nation to the largest debtor.

• Interest on the national debt is now more than 15 percent of all government expenditures. Interest payments are 35 percent higher than expenditures for drug control, crime control, the environment, research, roads, bridges, education, and all other federal programs except defense and entitlements.

• The increase in deficits, debt, and interest is due to federal expenditure growth (especially during the 1980s) having exceeded the growth in federal revenues and the growth in the CPI. Expenses, not revenues, are the problem.

• Entitlement programs have grown from 32 percent to 47 percent of all federal expenditures in the past twenty years. Interest on the national debt has grown from 7 percent to 15 percent, defense expenditures have been reduced from 45 percent to 27 percent and all other expenditures have dropped from 16 percent to 11 percent.

• Many entitlement costs are "out of control" because of COLA payments and lack of political will to make difficult changes.

• Social Security "surplus funds" should not be counted to show a smaller deficit, but should be channeled to enhance productivity and to help grow the economy.

• Consideration should be given to taxing Social Security benefits, reducing, delaying, or otherwise changing the COLAs and introducing some "means testing" and otherwise changing eligibility.

• As to Medicare, consideration should be given to the same kinds of changes suggested for Social Security, as appropriate, including some "means testing" for eligibility.

• The Military and Civil Service Retirement systems also deserve further cost reduction study.

• Budget deficits, national debt, and interest on the debt must be attacked more vigorously without precipitating adverse economic effects.

• With budget deficits eliminated, IRAs should be expanded to encourage savings and medical IRAs should be introduced.

• The federal economic pie should be more equitably distributed, with greater emphasis on need and improvements in air, water, roads, bridges, crime control, drug control, homelessness, and other serious national problems.

Clearly, the trend lines are not good; past actions have been weak, and the challenges are great. Still, I am enough of an optimist to believe that one way or another we will fight our way out of the dilemma we face—but strong warning signs are there and we ignore them at our peril!

NOTES

1. Office of Management and Budget, *Historical Tables: Budget of the United States Government Fiscal Year 1990* [hereinafter O.M.B. 1990 Budget].

2. U.S. Treasury, *Final Monthly Treasury Statement of Receipts and Outlays for Fiscal Year 1989* (Sept. 30, 1989) [hereinafter U.S. Treasury 1989 Statement]; Office of Management and Budget, *Historical Tables: Budget of the United States Government Fiscal Year 1987;* Office of Management and Budget, *Historical Tables: Budget of the United States Government Fiscal Year 1988.*

3. Congressional Budget Office projections of March 1990.

4. O.M.B. 1990 Budget; U.S. Treasury 1989 Statement.

5. O.M.B. 1990 Budget.

6. Ibid.

7. Ibid.

8. U.S. Dept. of Commerce, *Survey of Current Business* (June 1989).

9. O.M.B. 1990 Budget.

10. O.M.B. 1990 Budget; U.S. Treasury 1989 Statement.

11. O.M.B. 1990 Budget.

12. Congressional Budget Office, *The Economic and Budget Outlook: Fiscal Years 1990–1994* (Jan. 1989).

13. U.S. Treasury 1989 Statement.

14. As used herein, Social Security refers to the Old-Age, Survivors, and Disability Insurance program (OASDI).

15. Social Security Administration, *1989 OASDI Trustees Report* (Apr. 24, 1989) [hereinafter S.S.A. OASDI 1989 Report].

16. Ibid.

17. Metropolitan Life estimate.

18. Myers and Schobel, *A Money's-Worth Analysis of Social Security Retirement Benefits.* XXXV Transactions of the Society of Actuaries 542 (1983).

19. S.S.A. OASDI 1989 Report.

20. Ibid.

21. S.S.A. OASDI 1989 Report; Social Security Administration, *1988 HI Trustees Report* (May 5, 1988) [hereinafter S.S.A. HI 1988 Report]. For purposes of calculating the payroll tax rate, SMI is assumed to grow at the same rate as HI.

22. S.S.A. OASDI 1989 Report.

23. Office of Management and Budget, *The Budget for Fiscal Year 1991* (Jan. 29, 1990).

24. Haanes-Olsen, *Investment of Social Security Reserves in Three Countries,* 53 Social Security Bulletin (1990).

25. Social Security Administration, *1989 HI Trustees Report* (Dec. 5, 1989) [hereinafter S.S.A. HI 1989 Report]; Social Security Administration, *1989 SMI Trustees Report* (Apr. 24, 1989).

26. Employers and employees each pay a 1.45 percent payroll tax to fund the HI program.

27. S.S.A. HI 1988 Report.

28. Health Care Financing Administration, *Health Care Financing Review* (Supp. 1989); U.S. Dept. of Commerce, *U.S. Industrial Outlook 1990–Health Services* (Jan. 1990).

29. Schieber and Poullier, *International Health Care Expenditure Trends: 1987,* 8 Health Affairs 169 (Fall 1989).

30. Organization for Economic Cooperation and Development, *Measuring Health Care 1960–83* (1985).

31. The World Bank, *World Development Report: 1989* (June 1989).

32. Metropolitan Life estimate.

33. Department of Defense–Office of the Actuary, *Valuation of the Military Retirement System* (Sept. 30, 1988); U.S. Office of Personnel Management, unpublished data (Apr. 1990).

34. Ibid.

35. Ibid.

36. P. Peterson and N. Howe, *On Borrowed Time,* 321 (1988).

37. Organization for Economic Cooperation and Development and U.S. Dept. of Commerce.

38. Peterson and Howe, *On Borrowed Time,* 401.

39. U.S. Dept. of Commerce, Bureau of the Census, *Current Population Reports–Money Income and Poverty Status in the United States: 1987* 28 (Aug. 1988).

40. Metropolitan Life extrapolation based on a linear regression of 1969–1989 spending patterns; O.M.B. 1990 Budget.

41. Congressional Budget Office, *Reducing the Deficit: Spending and Revenue Options* (Feb. 1990).

42. Ibid.

43. Ibid.

I would like to thank some of my MetLife associates for helping with this project. Mr. Nicholas D. Latrenta, Vice-President, Mr. Robert H. Vatter, Vice-President and Economist, and Ms. Clara Cortes, Ms. April Hawkins, and Mr. Fred Creavin of MetLife's Corporate Issues Management staff provided valuable assistance in preparing and publishing the 1990 Lubin Lecture.

KEEPING AMERICA'S OPTIONS OPEN: THE KEY TO FUTURE ENERGY ABUNDANCE

Allen E. Murray

Chairman and Chief Executive Officer
Mobil Corporation

Essay by Allen E. Murray
on the occasion of the annual
Joseph I. Lubin Memorial Lecture
15 February 1989

Leonard N. Stern School of Business
New York University

I must confess that when I got my bachelor's degree from NYU, going on thirty-three years ago, I never dreamed I would stand here to address such a distinguished audience. Your kind invitation has made me proud and deeply grateful for the opportunity not only to be heard, but to listen to your comments and questions afterward.

The topic Dean Diamond originally suggested for this lecture was "Is an Energy Shortage on the Horizon?" Naturally, like good planners, we first had to define the word "horizon." We decided that the year 2000—only eleven years away—would provide a handy frame of reference. We also concluded that what would be valid for the year 2000 would probably remain true for at least several years beyond.

Then we consulted our corporate crystal ball, admittedly as cloudy as the next person's. It flashed a simple answer to Dean Diamond's question: No, there need not be an energy shortage. America—and, indeed, the world—has many energy options. If all the options are kept open and explored, the future will be one of energy abundance.

But there is a caveat. As our energy choices are considered, and as decisions are made, they should reflect good, hard economic sense. America has attained its leadership position in the world because of its economic might. In the final analysis, America can remain a premier political power in the next century only if it remains a premier economic power. And ample energy, at a reasonable price, is crucial to a strong economy.

Against that background, consider the wealth of energy sources available worldwide: oil, natural gas, and coal, as well as nuclear, solar, and geothermal sources. As we move toward the latter part of our time frame, perhaps fusion will be added to the list. Right now, oil provides some 43 percent of the energy consumed in the U.S. Coal provides 24 percent, natural gas 23 percent, and nuclear fuel 6 percent, with all other sources adding up to 4 percent. The statistics are similar for the free world as a whole.

I doubt the mix will change radically in eleven years. But it will not remain static, either. Crude oil and natural gas increasingly will be put to their high-value uses—those for which there are no ready substitutes. For oil, this means its use in transportation fuels. The high-value uses of natural gas are in petrochemical feedstocks and as the cleanest fuel available for most small consumers.

A single statistic will clearly define the importance of oil: Americans alone use about 20 percent of the free world's oil production to move our cars, trucks, planes, and other forms of transport. But America will never again be self-sufficient in crude oil. That is a fact of life we share with most of the industrialized nations of the free world. Japan imports virtually all its oil; the Western European nations are net importers, even though Great Britain and Norway are major producers.

Another fact of life is that the largest reserves are located in the Middle East. The OPEC nations produce better than 40 percent of the free world's oil and own two-thirds of the reserves. Furthermore, that's where most of the undiscovered reserves will be found in the future—and produced at lower cost than anywhere else in the world.

So the question for consuming nations, including the United States, isn't one of resources. Rather, it's how to assure continued access to this vital supply. The answer, I think, lies within the realms of normal diplomacy and normal trade relations.

Diplomacy should be viewed as the medium for attaining peace and stability in a notoriously unstable part of the world. That's a job for statesmen and political leaders. It surely won't be an easy job. But it must not be shrugged off as impossible. After all, who could have predicted such "impossible" events as an opening to China by a conservative U.S. president, or a peace treaty between Israel and Egypt, or the current thaw in U.S.-Soviet relations?

Trade relations should prove a lot easier. Everybody knows that buying OPEC oil adds to America's trade deficit. But hardly anybody realizes that the OPEC nations also buy a vast amount of merchandise from us. Last year, for example, the United States spent almost $23.5 billion in purchases from OPEC, virtually all of it for oil. But the OPEC countries bought almost $14 billion worth of merchandise from us—and that did not include services, like engineering, consulting, construction, computerization, insurance, and banking.

I firmly believe that the more the producing countries buy from the consuming countries, the more they will want to buy. Trade begets trade, and eventually the oil producers will become as dependent on the consuming countries as we are on them. Interdependence makes for stability, not only economically, but politically as well.

But will prices soar as supplies tighten in the next century and the world turns increasingly to OPEC oil? Again, I can only guess. But the producers do seem to have learned from experience. The sky-high prices of the 1970s led to an intensive search for non-OPEC oil and to major discoveries in places like the North Sea and off eastern Canada, to name just two. And those same high prices forced the world to adopt conservation measures that are now part of the infrastructure: better-insulated homes and offices, more efficient cars, and factories able to switch fuels at will. These same factors helped produce today's oil glut and low prices—developments that hardly escaped OPEC. In other words, I do not think prices will collapse during our time frame, and neither do I think they will soar.

If the worldwide oil trade is allowed to function normally, the fact that America imports 40 percent or even 50 percent or more of its oil is no cause for alarm. But what if stability cannot be achieved? What if, because of some political or terrorist act, access to these vital reserves is interdicted?

There are several insurance policies available to America and the free world. International machinery already exists for cooperation among consuming nations. In the United States, our own production plus the Strategic Petroleum Reserve (SPR) should see us through a brief supply interruption. The SPR now contains over half a billion barrels. That is enough to replace our net imports for ninety days at today's import levels. The SPR is targeted for three-quarters of a billion barrels, and I would like to see it grow further as imports grow. If the SPR had existed in the seventies, there's no question that we would not have experienced gasoline lines.

Remember, the world has never experienced an oil supply interruption that lasted more than a few months. I am convinced the world never will—it simply would not be tolerated. Even so, I am equally convinced that America ought to find and produce all the economic domestic oil it can—not because of any national security concerns, but because it makes good business sense.

While there's nothing intrinsically wrong with importing oil, every dollar we lop off our import bill is a dollar off our trade deficit. And cutting the trade deficit is definitely good for the country. But too often politics get in the way. As an example, let's look at Alaska. The Prudhoe Bay field there, America's largest, has been producing for over ten years. It is currently yielding something like a million and a half barrels a day—almost a fifth of America's total production. But it is already entering its inevitable period of decline.

Less than a hundred miles away, along the Beaufort Sea coastal plain, lies the Arctic National Wildlife Refuge, an area of some nineteen million acres —about the size of New Hampshire, Vermont, Connecticut, and Massachusetts combined. A small portion of these lands—some million and a half acres—have been identified as having good oil potential. In fact, Interior Department data indicate it could be the site of the largest field remaining to be found onshore in the United States.

But drilling in Alaska has become embroiled in a lengthy dispute. It is as if economic development and a clean environment are black-and-white concepts, beyond reconciliation. And that is unfortunate, because both can certainly be achieved together.

The oil industry's positive safety record in Prudhoe Bay and the successful coexistence of caribou and the Alaskan pipeline prove the point. Even so, controversy rages, development is stalled, and few people worry, because oil is cheap and oil is plentiful—and the trade deficit is an esoteric concept.

Similar controversies erupt whenever the industry attempts to drill offshore California, and even offshore the Atlantic coast, where the success rate to date has been zero and where only a few companies have even the wish to explore. Here, too, the economic arguments ought to be carefully heeded. And the same kind of economic considerations must color the decision we eventually make about our other energy options.

The nation has large reserves of natural gas. But making the best use of them means continuing the process of price decontrol. It also means further progress in providing producers with open access to pipelines, so they can best respond to the direct needs of the consumer. These are economic decisions. They need to be depoliticized. America's coal supplies are also huge. But burning coal is becoming increasingly enmeshed in environmental arguments—especially as scientists debate whether or not there is indeed a greenhouse effect and, if there is, what has to be done about it.

The nuclear industry is in complete disarray in America—there has not been a new plant proposed in about ten years. Meanwhile, the French, the Japanese, and even the Russians—in spite of Chernobyl—are proceeding with their programs. America has to decide how much of its electricity it wants to generate through nuclear power. And it has to weigh the costs and environmental impact against the costs and environmental impact of using oil, gas, and coal—again, economic decisions.

Even gasoline is coming in for harsh criticism in the name of environmentalism. There are proposals to mandate the use of alcohol fuels, especially in those parts of the country that have not attained compliance with federal clean air standards. Now I don't quarrel with experimenting with alcohol fuels and I certainly don't quarrel with clean air. Mobil used to sell gasohol, a blend of ethanol and gasoline. But mandating alcohol use is another issue. There is genuine concern over whether such fuels really do cut pollution, and there is even some evidence that certain of them may increase ozone formation. Besides, alcohols simply are not economic right now. And they are not likely to be in the future, without subsidies. Does the country need more subsidies to add to the budget deficit?

What America does need is a national debate and a national consensus on energy policy. The time to hammer out such a consensus and such a policy is now, when there's plenty of energy around and prices are low. Gasoline lines of the sort we experienced in the seventies are not conducive to rational action.

Don't get me wrong. I'm definitely not predicting gasoline lines. In fact, the whole thrust of my thesis is that we do have plenty of options and that we have only to decide how to use them.

We have something else going for us as well— the increasing array of energy technology at our command. Our American oil field technology remains the envy of the world and is being exported all over the world. We inject water, steam, and chemicals to extract more and more oil from old fields. Our sophisticated computers can create models that define a field's dimensions with more precision than we have ever had before. We have found new reservoirs beneath existing fields, where we never thought to drill before. Space satellites now help us to decide where to drill, and we know more about potential prospects than we ever did before. And energy technology extends beyond exploration and production. Modern U.S. refineries can upgrade heavier, higher-sulfur crudes—precisely the types we will have to rely on increasingly in the future.

A university discussion like ours today is a logical forum for citing our technological prowess. Increasingly, energy companies will need the engineers, geologists, geophysicists, computer specialists, and others who will keep stretching the boundaries of knowledge. Only the universities can provide them. But universities need to go further. Companies also need liberal arts and business graduates who, like professionals, can think—and who can learn all during their careers. They are the people who will—in conjunction with government and the public at large—implement the decisions and carry out the consensus we need. And they will have to sort through and prioritize America's need for economic strength even as they maintain and enhance the environment in which all of us live together.

America needs a strong economy to maintain its leadership role. Leadership, after all, is economic strength.

Let me sum up. An energy shortage into the next century is not a probability. Not if we examine all our options and put them to work.

Not if we allow the nation's business sector to engage in the kind of free and fair trade that binds nations together—and minimizes differences.

Not if government provides the leadership and the environment that allow this process to unfold.

Not if our colleges and universities provide us with the talent we need to retain our technological strengths, our management skills, and our economic might.

And certainly not, if all of us become an active part of the process of debate and consensus making —and begin that process today.

For if we do all these things, and do them well, we may even find ourselves with an energy surplus. That would mean stable prices and a multiplicity of choices—which is not exactly a bad legacy to leave the generations of Americans to come.

QUESTION AND ANSWER

Mr. Murray, you spoke of options we have in fuel; you spoke of alcohol. . . . What is your opinion of shale?

Well, we have a number of options in the country today; let me take them all, including shale. You've got solar. There's no mystery to it. We can convert sunlight directly into electricity. It's just not in the ball park economically. Coal—we can convert the vast reserves of coal we have in this nation into natural gas, into methanol, and into gasoline. We have a process now—Mobil does, a Mobil process in New Zealand—where we take natural gas and convert it effectively through stages into gasoline. It can be done, but not yet economically. As for shale, the reserves exist. We can turn them into oil and then refine it like any other oil. It's just not economic. The alternative energy sources are not going to be a factor economically in the next twenty years, in my opinion, but we can do them all.

What is your view of import fees as a solution to our energy problems?

I don't like import fees. I don't like anything that gets the government back into businesses it shouldn't be in. I think the oil import fee is counterproductive. It doesn't do anything. I don't think this industry should be asking for protection at this stage, which, besides raising some revenues, is effectively what an import fee is designed to do. I think it's a terrible mistake. We don't have a lot of company, maybe, but we are vehemently opposed to an import fee. I think it's wrong for the country.

Are you concerned that we are importing a larger percentage of oil today than at the time of the OPEC embargo in the 1970s? Doesn't this adversely affect U.S. national security?

What security? Are you going to feel more secure if you're 40 percent dependent on imports rather than 50? If you just look at energy self-sufficiency, Japan has no security. This national security argument, in my opinion, is the most overblown thing I've ever heard. If you were telling me I was going from 92 percent to 100 percent self-sufficiency and I could thumb my nose at the world, I'd say you're probably not very bright to do it, but I could understand an argument of national security. You want national security, I'll tell you what to do—and you won't like this, nobody does: We drill up in Alaska, let's say, and we find a five billion-barrel field. We spend all the money. We put the wells in and don't pump it. That's national security. It's there when you want it. To bring a field on, run it down, make

money—which I love—and call it national security
—I'm sorry. It isn't. What I am saying is—these
are economic decisions. There are two words that
we have to worry about, two phrases: environment
and national security. Because when a person uses
those words, we don't know what they mean; they
are important, but misused.

*Based upon your answer to the first question, what
do you see in terms of the timetable for developing
an economic alternative to the automobile?*

If you're talking pure economics without subsidies,
I don't see anything in the time frame we're talking
about in any major way. Let's say fifteen years.
Then you'll ask: Are there going to be electric cars?
Is someone going to invent something new? . . . But
if you invent something tomorrow that nobody has,
it would take you that long to make a major dent
with it, so I don't see it on the horizon. You're
going to see silly things done; you're going to see
alcohol fuels. And everybody's going to say they're
the greatest thing since ice cream, but they're not
going to make any sense. You're going to pay for
them as the taxpayer; you're not even going to know

you're paying for them. A couple of guys are going to get rich. But I really don't see much else happening in fifteen years.

How seriously do you view Third World debt?

Well, of course, it's very, very serious. It's serious because of the impact it has on their economies and the world's economy and the banking fraternity and everybody else. Also, we have a concern about the political ramifications within those very countries. So I think it's very severe. Obviously they can't pay the debt back now, and they're going to have to be forgiven. Many of those nations are coming back, I think. It hasn't impacted very much on us. The banking people probably know a lot more than I do. I think it's a very serious matter. Do I think the whole region is suddenly going to go communist because of it? No, I don't. Do I think we're going to have to stretch those loans out? Yes, we are. But I hope the government of the United States doesn't start picking them up.

Would you be kind enough to give us an outlook on the refining business?

Yes, it looks great right now in the United States. "Great" is a relative term. It hasn't been so good for many years. It looks very good now. What has happened is that the refining capacity is utilized up around 90 percent—give or take. But when you take the upgrading portion, the gasoline-making portion, and you allow for the normal downtime of refineries, it's running at near capacity. . . . Now I'm talking United States; Europe is a different ball game, . . . but in the United States the refineries are making it. We bought one at the end of last year, and my stockholders obviously think we made the right decision. We wouldn't have bought one if we didn't think it was good. In Europe, it's a little different. Europe still has a surplus of refining capacity, and so, while things are looking a little better, they're still not healthy.

Mr. Murray, you mentioned the need for talent—especially for the future—in identifying new energy sources and managing the problems. Do you see the nation's business schools as a whole producing the talent that we will need in the future, or do you see them producing the type of money-grubbing people that they have a reputation for?

I think that the business schools and the universities generally in the United States are doing an outstanding job. I think the problem we're having in education in this country is at the lower level. I really think we're not equipping people, going back to the grammar schools and the high schools. I don't think students are being prepared. I have been associated with some university graduates (not from NYU) who have business degrees and can't write. They can think, but they can't communicate. If you get a piece of paper from them, the ideas don't come through, and if they do, they take up thirty pages where they should need a page and a half. That's a problem. But let me talk about education generally in the universities. This nation faces a very, very serious, critical situation. And I'm not talking about elementary school education now. What I'm talking about is the demographics of our work force. We have dramatically changing demographics. The day of the white male entry worker is over, it's finished, it's gone, goodbye. The work force coming in is increasingly female and minority. That's a fact of life. But the problem we have is, for reasons that I'm not sure I can explain, these people are not taking the technical disciplines. We have a major problem if we're going to keep up with all of the countries around the world. You find that very few women, relative to white males, go into the technical disciplines. When they do, they do fine, but they don't go in. We've got to somehow make them understand that being an engineer doesn't mean you have to be under a truck fixing something. It is a business function. Blacks offer a worse example: a very low percentage going into the technical skills and about half of them leaving before they finish. It's a serious problem in this country. We can't turn suddenly into a service country where we're passing papers back and forth. Now these are questions I don't know the answers to, but I surely think with all the brains in this university, maybe you can figure it out. Because it really is a major, major problem. It's an opportunity, but it's a problem right now. The rosters of the engineering schools, of the technical schools—there are just not many women and blacks and Hispanics. As an American, I am very concerned.

AFTERWORD

Daniel E. Diamond

Dean, The Undergraduate College
Leonard N. Stern School of Business
New York University

The Stern School of Business is one of the oldest and most respected schools of business in this country and the world. Founded in 1900 by Charles Waldo Haskins as the School of Commerce, Accounts, and Finance, it pioneered in the development of professional accounting education at the collegiate level. Since virtually all of its enrollees were part-time students, it opened satellite programs in a number of locations in the New York City/metropolitan area, including the Wall Street financial district. By World War I there were enough baccalaureate graduates who were interested in advanced work to initiate a graduate degree program. In 1916, the School of Commerce's Wall Street branch became the home of New York University's Graduate School of Business Administration (GBA).

By the 1920s, the School of Commerce's programs were sufficiently broad to warrant the awarding of the Bachelor of Science degree. It was the first business school to do so. In the 1920s and 1930s, the School experienced continued growth in both the quality and breadth of its programs of study. The post–World War II period was one of unprecedented growth in the number of students at the School of Commerce and the Graduate School of Business Administration, as both veterans and high school graduates chose business school in record numbers.

In the 1960s, following the publication of the Ford and Carnegie Foundations' critical studies of collegiate business education, both Commerce and GBA fundamentally restructured their respective missions. Admissions and faculty hiring, promotion and tenure standards—all were raised. Henceforth, all business majors were built on a solid liberal arts base. Programs of study were refocused to stress conceptual and analytical material. Wherever possible they were related to the appropriate arts and science discipline.

In the 1970s, reflecting its new curriculum and outlook, the School of Commerce was renamed the College of Business and Public Administration

(BPA). At the same time, it moved to new, modern quarters in its present home—Tisch Hall. To strengthen its research and teaching, the faculty of BPA and GBA were merged into a joint Faculty of Business at New York University, simultaneously serving both undergraduate and graduate students.

In 1985, the Faculty of Business embarked on the formulation of a strategic, long-range plan. In 1987, it approved a major reorientation and restructuring of New York University's business schools. A year later, after receiving endorsements from the university's central administration and board of trustees, the plan was launched. At the same time, the university announced a $30 million gift to the business schools by Leonard N. Stern, an alumnus of both the School of Commerce and the Graduate School of Business Administration, as well as a trustee of the university. In recognition of Mr. Stern's extraordinary benefaction, the trustees renamed the business schools the Leonard N. Stern School of Business with an undergraduate college and a graduate division. Mr. Stern is the chief executive officer of the Hartz Group, Inc. His gift, thus far, is the largest single contribution to support collegiate business education in the United States.

The long-range plan is a comprehensive educational effort to create uncompromising academic excellence in all phases of the Stern School's activities. In so doing, it will enable the school's graduates to better meet the daunting demands of leadership in the 1990s and the twenty-first century beyond. Its major components include:

1. The consolidation of the faculty and the graduate and undergraduate divisions in a new, state-of-the-art, three-building Management Education Center at the university's main Washington Square campus. Occupancy will begin in the fall of 1992.
2. A 20 percent reduction in the student body at both the undergraduate and graduate levels with a concomitant improvement in the student/faculty ratio.
3. A refocusing of the MBA program to increase the relative importance of the full-time component and to stabilize part-time enrollment at two thousand students.
4. A strengthening of the core curriculum at both the graduate and undergraduate levels to provide more work in management communications, business ethics and values, globalization, the

historical perspective, and operations management.

5. A change in hiring, promotion, and tenure standards to bring teaching and education up to the same level of importance as research.
6. The adoption of a quality standard for the classroom presentation skills of the faculty.
7. The consolidation of the graduate division's library collections with the existing volumes at the university's main Bobst Library to create a world class business research and reference library.

Presently, the Stern School's graduate division is consistently rated by both *Business Week* and *U.S. News and World Report* as one of the nation's top twenty business schools. For many years, its undergraduate college has been included in the top ten list by *The Gourman Report*. The long-range plan has the potential to further improve the Stern School rankings.

Despite the many changes envisioned by the plan, the Stern School will continue its many proud traditions. These include producing outstanding business leaders (Standard and Poors's biennial survey of the top executives at America's major corporations lists New York University's Stern School of Business as second only to Harvard in terms of where these individuals earned their degrees); being a school of opportunity at the undergraduate level for immigrants and the sons and daughters of immigrants; and serving as a forum for the discussion of the leading economic, financial, and management issues of the day, as evidenced by the lectures and conferences sponsored by the Lubin Memorial Lecture Series, the Center for Japan/U.S. Business and Economic Studies, the NYU/Salomon Center for the Study of Financial Institutions, and the Petrie Lectures in Entrepreneurship.

DATE DUE

HIGHSMITH #45230

Printed
in USA